National Park Service
U.S. Department of the Interior

Fire Island National Seashore
Fire Island, New York

Fire Island National Seashore
Survey of Walk- in Visitors

PMIS No. 63642
April 2005

John A. Volpe National Transportation Systems Center
Research and Innovative Technology Administration
U.S. Department of Transportation

Contents

Report notes

This report was prepared by the U.S. Department of Transportation John A. Volpe National Transportation Systems Center, in Cambridge, Massachusetts. Michael G. Dyer, of the Technology Applications and Deployment Division lead the project team. Robert Armstrong and Judith C. Schwenk of the Service and Operations Assessment Division were senior analysts providing statistical and operational support. Deirdre Carrigan of the Technology Applications and Deployment Division assisted in data entry.

This effort was undertaken in fulfillment of PMIS 63642, *Fire Island Ferry Route Plans, Phase II*. It continues work initiated and documented in the February 2001 Phase I report, *Fire Island National Seashore Waterborne Transportation System Plan*, in which the Volpe Center identified ferry and water taxi service and terminal improvements to be phased in from 2001- 2010, and outlined additional planning, analysis, and design work to support facility and ferry services development, elements of which are addressed by this scope of work. The project statement of work was conducted in cooperation with the Federal Highway Administration (FHWA) under Volpe Center/FHWA Project Plan Agreement HW1M as a supplement to PMIS 63642.

Acknowledgments

The following individuals graciously provided their time, knowledge and guidance in the development of this survey report:

National Park Service
Robert Holzheimer
Lou DeLorme
Robert Forist

Fire Island National Seashore
Constantine Dillon, Superintendent
Maria Abonnel
Steve Henderson
Libby Schaaf

Fire Island National Seashore Volunteers
Betty Berman
Jessica Cunn
Marlies Knies
Carl and JoAnn Latenza
Wes Mudford

Definitions

The following acronyms are used in this report:

DOT   Department of Transportation
FHWA   Federal Highway Administration
FI   Fire Island
FINS   Fire Island National Seashore
NPS   National Park Service
OMB   Office of Management and Budget

Section 1: Introduction

Fire Island National Seashore is located on Fire Island, a 32- mile long barrier island along the southern coast of Long Island. Its beaches and lands, interwoven with the island's many residential communities, are visited primarily during the summer months by between three and four million people each year. The lack of conventional ground transport modes and services presents a challenge to visitors, who must come by either ferry or private boat, or walk in from neighboring communities and state and county parks.

Purpose of survey

In 2000 the Fire Island National Seashore (FINS) embarked on a two- phase study of Fire Island ferry route plans. Phase I produced the February 2001 report *FINS Waterborne Transportation System Plan*[*] based on the August 2000 FINS Ferry Transportation Survey. In July 2002 two more surveys were conducted as part of Phase II: the Survey of Walk- in Visitors[†] and the Lateral Ferry Survey. This report documents the Survey of Walk- in Visitors. The Lateral Ferry Survey is documented in a separate report (NPS TIC No. D- 96).

The FINS Survey of Walk- in Visitors was conducted with the aim of determining how public access to the island can be improved. This survey obtained input from visitors who access the National Seashore on foot from nearby Robert Moses State Park on the East End of FINS and Smith Point County Park on the West End. The information will aid FINS in further developing its waterborne transportation plan for the improvement of public access to, and use and enjoyment of, FINS resources.

Seashore description

Fire Island is a narrow barrier island 32 miles in length along the south coast of Long Island, separating Great South Bay from the Atlantic Ocean and includes the authorized areas of the National Seashore, Robert Moses State Park, Smith Point County Park, and private lands in several residential communities. FINS includes the Otis Pike High Dunes Wilderness Area, Watch Hill, Talisman/Barrett Beach, Sailors Haven, and Fire Island Lighthouse; the small islands of East Fire Island and West Fire Island; and parks run by the towns of Brookhaven and Islip.

Fire Island National Seashore consists of ocean beaches, dunes, maritime forests, and significant portions of the Great South Bay and Moriches Bay. Located approximately one hour east of New York City, Fire Island is a popular destination for ocean beach recreation, sightseeing, hiking and wildlife viewing. Camping is allowed is designated areas, and the coastal location provides opportunities for canoeing, boating and fishing.

The residential communities on Fire Island have a combined summer resident population of approximately 30,000, which is reduced to only 450 during the off- season winter months. Although most areas of the park are open year- round, visitation is highly seasonal, with the vast majority of visitation generally occurring during the summer months. Automobile use on the island is prohibited during the summer when visitation is highest, and is allowed only under restricted conditions during the off- peak winter season when ferry operations are reduced.

Because the use of motor vehicles is restricted on the island, approximately 80 to 90 percent of the estimated 3 to 4 million annual visitors to the federally- managed portions of Fire Island access the Island by either ferry or private boat. Visitors can also access the island by driving over bridges to

---

[*] *Fire Island National Seashore Waterborne Transportation System Plan*, by the Volpe Center for NPS FINS, February 2001.

[†] Originally scheduled for August 2000, the Visitor Survey had to be postponed for logistical reasons. The Office of Management and Budget (OMB) extended its original survey approval to accommodate the July 2002 survey period, as required by the Paperwork Reduction Act of 1995.

parking areas located in Robert Moses State Park and Smith Point County Park, and then walking to the federally managed portions of the Island.

The National Park Service wishes to encourage greater use of park facilities during the off-season non-summer months. FINS staff believe that enhancement of alternative transportation services can help facilitate access to the resources of Fire Island, and support the needs of year-round residents, seasonal renters, and day visitors.

Report structure

Section 1 introduces the report with a statement of the survey purpose and a description of the attributes of the Fire Island and National Seashore.

Section 2 describes the Visitor Survey methodology, including the survey instrument, respondent universe, sampling plan and procedures, and survey administration.

Section 3 presents the survey results, including a description of the survey's implementation, response, data editing and analysis, and findings.

Section 4 provides a summary of the survey methodology and findings.

Appendix A contains the NPS expedited survey approval form and Appendix B contains the script for surveyors in addressing potential respondents.

Figure 1
Map of Fire Island
Source: *Fire Island Official Map and Guide*, National Park Service, U.S. Department of the Interior

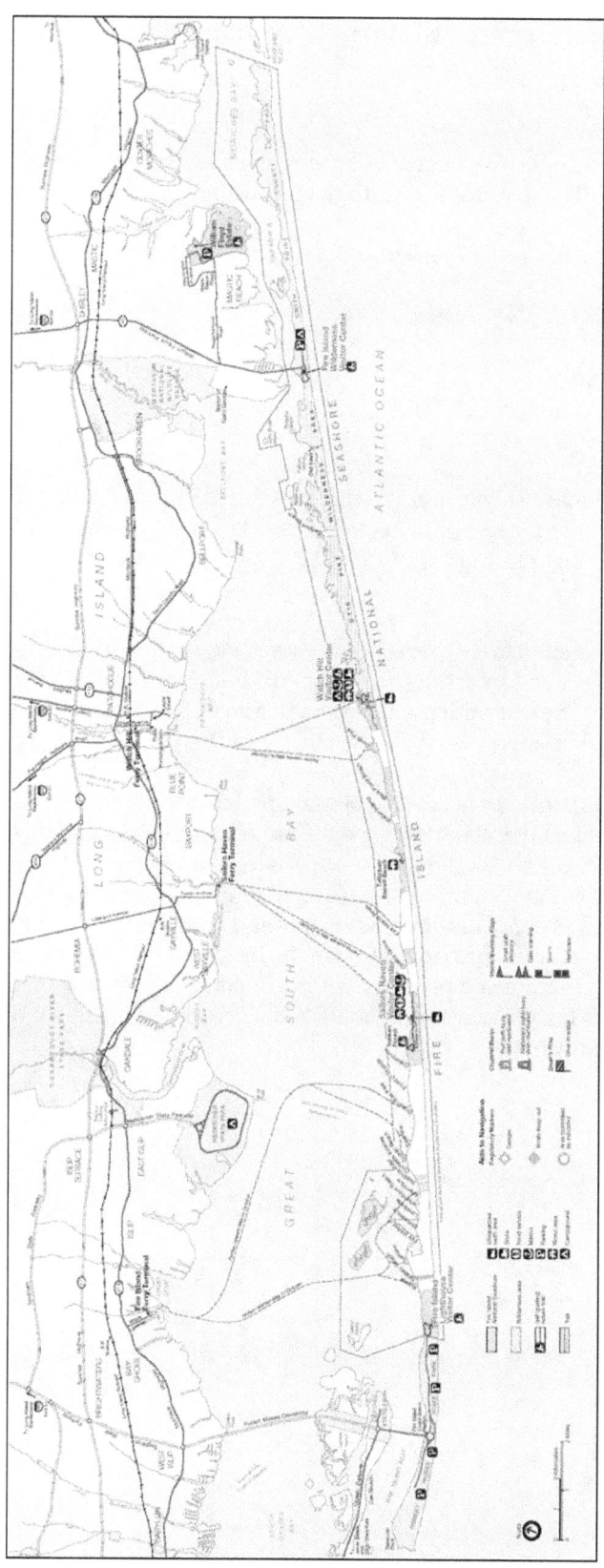

Section 2: Survey methodology

This section discusses describes the Visitor Survey methodology[*], including the survey instrument, respondent universe, sampling plan and procedures, and survey administration.

Survey instrument

The Visitor Survey instrument contained 12 questions and was estimated to take about five minutes for a visitor to complete. The questions fell into the following topic areas:

- Individual perception of FINS experiences

- Individual evaluation of FINS services

- Trip/visit characteristics

- Individual characteristics

The surveys were printed on a single, double-sided 8.5 x 11 inch page, using a heavy weight card stock paper to make it easier for respondents to handle. The front and back of the survey instrument are shown in Figures 2 and 3.

Respondent universe

This survey aimed to characterize the views of the survey population, that is, of all visitors age 18 and older who access FINS on foot from either Robert Moses State Park to the West or Smith Point County Park to the East. The respondent universe consisted of all those visitors with the potential of being sampled for the survey.

In order to minimize the resources needed to obtain the desired information and maximize the responses, it was determined that the survey would occur on one weekend day during the summer season, as weekends have the heaviest patterns of visitation to FINS and the nearby state and county parks. As park personnel believed that there was no significant systematic variation in the characteristics of the visitor populations on Saturdays and Sundays, implementing the survey on a single Sunday would produce a representative sample. In addition, the large number of weekend visitors would represent a significant potential source of patronage for alternative travel modes, such as new or improved ferry services, that could be used by FINS visitors who currently drive and park in the state and county parks.

---

[*] Appendix A contains the FINS Visitor Survey approval package with a thorough description of the survey methodology, submitted to OMB under the Paperwork Reduction Act of 1995.

Fire Island National Seashore Visitor Survey

OMB Control Number 1024-0224 Expiration Date: 01/31/2003	NPS Identification Number NPS00-034

This survey is being conducted by the National Park Service in cooperation with Robert Moses State Park and Smith Point County Park to help determine how access to Fire Island can be improved. Please help us by answering as many questions as you can.   **THANK YOU**

Please answer some questions about _this_ visit to Fire Island:

(1) Fire Island is a National Seashore (a unit of the National Park System). Were you aware that you are entering a National Seashore? (check one only)
❏ Yes   ❏ No

(2) How many people, including yourself, are in your traveling party today?: _____

(3) Why did you choose to access the National Seashore by foot rather than taking a ferry to another area of the National Seashore?

❏ Fares too high on existing ferry routes
❏ Existing ferry routes don't serve desired locations
❏ Preferred to drive my own car
❏ Other reason (please specify): _____
_____
_____

(4) Why did you choose to visit the National Seashore instead of, or in addition to, Robert Moses State Park or Smith Point County Park?

❏ Access to more beach areas or better quality beach areas
❏ Access to more specific attractions (e.g., Otis Pike Wilderness Area, Fire Island Lighthouse, etc.)
❏ Other reason (please specify): _____
_____
_____

(5) Did you pay for parking today?
❏ Yes   ❏ No

(6) Were you aware that the funds you paid for parking do not go to the national seashore or to service the beach or other national seashore area you are using?
❏ Yes   ❏ No

Please answer some questions about yourself:

(7) What is the zip code where your permanent residence is located?: _____
If not a U.S. resident, in what country is your permanent residence located?: _____

(8) What are the ages of the persons in your traveling party (including yourself)?

Age Category =>	18 to 24	25 to 34	35 to 44	45 to 64	65 or over
Number of Persons =>					

(9) What is _your_ age? (check one only)

❏ 18 to 24   ❏ 25 to 34   ❏ 35 to 44   ❏ 45 to 64   ❏ 65 or over

(CONTINUED ON THE REVERSE SIDE) ➷

(CONTINUED FROM THE REVERSE SIDE)

(10) What is your gender? (check one only)

❑ *Male*   ❑ *Female*

(11) What is your annual household pre-tax income? (check one only)

(this information will be used for statistical purposes only)

❑ *Under $25,000*   ❑ *$50,000 to $74,999*   ❑ *$100,000 or more*

❑ *$25,000 to $49,999*   ❑ *$75,000 to $99,999*

(12) If <u>new</u> ferry routes serving National Seashore areas were to be introduced, what potential <u>new</u> ferry routes, if any, would you find desirable? (check all that apply - if no opinion leave all blank)

❑ No new routes needed, existing routes are sufficient   ❑ Patchogue - Barrett Beach
❑ Bay Shore - Fire Island Lighthouse   ❑ Patchogue - Fire Island Lighthouse
❑ Sayville - Fire Island Lighthouse   ❑ Heckscher State Park - Sailors Haven
❑ Heckscher State Park - Fire Island Lighthouse
❑ Coastwise (east-west) ferry service along Fire Island serving National Seashore areas (for example, Fire Island Lighthouse, Sailors Haven, Barrett Beach, Watch Hill)
❑ Other Route (please specify):_____

Additional Comments/Suggestions:

PAPER WORK REDUCTION ACT STATEMENT

Sample size and sampling procedures

On a typical weekend day during the peak visitation season, it was estimated that approximately 3,000 visitors the FINS access the park on foot from Robert Moses State Park to the West, and 1,500 visitors access FINS on foot from Smith Point County Park to the East. Of this total respondent universe of 4,500 visitors, a sample of 300 visitors (200 entering from the West and 100 entering from the East) would be selected throughout the day at access points along the beach and along the boardwalks, contacted by a FINS representative, and asked to participate in the survey. From past experience with surveys that intercept visitors as they enter the park ("intercept" surveys), a sample of 300 would be expected to produce about 150 completed responses, a response rate of 50 percent. Considered a "large" survey in statistical terms, this sample size would produce statistically significant results that reliably represented the walk- in visitor population. A systematic sampling approach would be used, in which every 15th person at each access point would be selected. There was no reason to believe that such a sampling order would be biased; therefore, this approach would essentially be equivalent to a simple random sample.

Figure 4
Survey location for intercepting visitors entering FINS from Robert Moses State Park via walkway
Source: Volpe Center

Survey administration

On the Sunday the survey was administered, there would be four survey field workers, two at the East End of FINS and two at the West End, one intercepting visitors gaining access to FINS along the beach and the other intercepting visitors gaining access to FINS along the boardwalk. Signs announcing the survey would be placed in strategic locations. Survey instruments would be secured to clip boards, and golf pencils would be provided to the respondents. Surveyors would collect the completed surveys.

Also planned was the recording of observable characteristics, such as gender, an estimate of group size and age, of visitors who declined to participate in the survey when approached. This would make it possible to determine any systematic distortion in survey responses might have occurred due to differences between the respondents and non- respondents. If substantial differences were found, the resulting information could be used to weight the survey responses to reflect more accurately the true views of the respondent universe.

Figure 5
Survey location for intercepting visitors entering FINS from Smith Point County Park via walkway
Source: Volpe Center

Section 2: Survey results

This section presents the survey results, including a description of the survey's implementation, response, data editing and analysis, and findings.

Survey implementation and response

Implementation
The Visitor Survey took place over two weekend days. Although the original plan was for the survey to be conducted on Sunday, July 28, 2002, the available resources and weather conspired to stretch it out over two days. FINS staff lined up citizen volunteers to administer the survey; however, there were only enough volunteers to conduct the Visitor Survey at one of the two locations at a time, and their time would have to be limited to several hours at each location. Splitting the survey into two days would not affect its validity, as both days were weekend days, and there was no reason to believe systematic differences existed between Saturday and Sunday visitors. The revised plan called for the survey to occur at the East End on Saturday, July 27, and the West End on Sunday, July 28.

An alteration of the revised plan occurred due to the poor weather conditions on Saturday. The clouds, cool temperature and occasional light drizzle discouraged visitors, and only 35 surveys were collected. Consequently, the ranger at the Wilderness Center distributed surveys on Sunday when he was not occupied with other official duties.

The weather also affected the way the survey was administered. Not only was the weather on Saturday poor, but also the weather on Sunday was less than ideal with heavy, fog for most of the day. To obtain as many responses as possible in their limited time on duty, surveyors approached almost all people approaching FINS on foot from the East and West Ends, rather than every 15th arrival as requested in the survey administration instructions. And they did not record information about those who refused to participate, due to their other responsibilities on the survey days. However, surveyors did report that visitors were very willing to cooperate in the survey and that there were only a handful of refusals.

Response
Table 1 shows the number of Visitor Survey responses by location and day. Fifty- six surveys were collected over the two day period at the East End and 136 on Sunday at the West End for a total of 192. As expected, the majority of surveys (70.8 percent) were collected near the Lighthouse in the West, as the number of visitors is greater at that location.

Table 1
Visitor Survey responses by day of week and location
Source: Volpe Center, FINS Visitor Survey

	East End	West End	Total
Saturday	35	--	35
Sunday	21	136	157
Total	56	136	192
Percent	29.2%	70.8%	100%

Although the circumstances of the Visitor Survey implementation preclude a quantitative assessment of response rate and bias, at least qualitatively according to the participating surveyors, the response rate was good, and there was no observable bias. The response rate of the companion Ferry Transportation Survey conducted in 2000 was 70.8 percent overall. Given parallel survey circumstances for the two (Ferry Survey prospects were approached as they were about to board a ferry; Visitor Survey prospects were approached as they headed for the beach), it would be reasonable to assume that visitor disposition had not changed dramatically over the two- year period and the Visitor Survey would produce a similar response rate to the Ferry Survey.

However, the degree to which people who are willing to go to the beach in less than ideal conditions differ from fair weather beachgoers may affect the general applicability of the survey results to all those who access FINS by foot. For example, it is possible that poor weather disproportionately discourages families with small children. Users of the survey results should take this into consideration.

Survey processing

Survey respondents completed a very high percentage of the questions on each survey. The question on income had the greatest number of missing answers, as expected, with 25 surveys leaving this field blank. Thirteen surveys were missing zip code. In the calculation of results, a blank field was treated as a non- response for a particular question and percentages were based only on the set of completed answers for that question.

As Question 8 on the ages of the persons in the travel party did not include a category for persons less than 18 years old, many respondents wrote in the number of young people in their party. In the analysis of results, a "< 18" category was added for the write- ins. This is somewhat problematic in the interpretation of the age data, as some respondents might have left out the number of people less than 18 years old because there was no place for them on the form. Therefore the number reported should be considered a lower bound for the true number of people less than 18 years old, and the actual age distribution skewed toward older ages.

Survey findings

Awareness of National Seashore

Question 1 on the survey form asked, *"Fire Island is a National Seashore (a unit of the National Park System). Were you aware that you are entering a National Seashore?"* Table 2 shows responses to this question. Overall over 92 percent of respondents walking into FINS were aware they were entering a National Seashore. Awareness at the Fire Island Lighthouse on the western end of Fire Island was extremely high at 96.3 percent, while the awareness at the Wilderness Area in the East, though high, stood at 82.1 percent.

Table 2
Respondent awareness of National Seashore
Source: Volpe Center, FINS Visitor Survey

Awareness		East End Visitors	West End Visitors	Total Visitors
Yes	Number	46	131	177
	% by Location	82.1%	96.3%	92.2%
No	Number	10	5	15
	% by Location	17.9%	3.7%	7.8%

Reason for arriving by foot

Table 3 shows the reasons respondents chose to access the National Seashore by foot rather than taking a ferry to another area of FINS. Question 3 on the survey form offered the choices of:

- Fares too high on existing ferry routes

- Existing ferry routes don't serve desired locations

- Preferred to drive my own car

- Other reason (please specify)

The vast majority of respondents at both the east and West Ends cited a preference for driving their own cars to the parking lots and walking in (61.8 percent in the East, 74.1 percent in the West, and 74.4 percent overall). West End respondents were over twice as likely to cite that ferry routes did not serve desired locations (16.3 percent) than East End respondents (7.3 percent). But East End respondents chose the high price of ferry fares more often than West End respondents as a reason for accessing FINS by foot (12.7 percent vs. 4.4 percent). About 13 percent of the respondents indicated in their comments that they were staying on Fire Island and walked in. Other reasons cited included biking in and coming on private boats.

Table 3
Reasons for accessing FINS by foot
Source: Volpe Center, FINS Visitor Survey

Percent of Responses by Reason*	East End Visitors	West End Visitors	Total Visitors
Preferred to drive own car	61.8%	74.1%	74.4%
Ferry routes don't serve desired locations	7.3%	16.3%	14.4%
Living/staying nearby	9.1%	13.3%	12.8%
Fares too high on existing routes	12.7%	4.4%	7.2%
Other	16.4%	7.4%	10.6%

* Note: Respondents could choose more than one reason.

Reasons for choosing FINS

Table 4 shows that respondents from the East and West Ends of FINS had very different reasons for choosing to visit FINS when given the following question: *"Why did you choose to visit the National Seashore instead of, or in addition to, Robert Moses State Park or Smith Point County Park?"*

- Access to more beach areas or better quality beach areas

- Access to more specific attractions (e.g., Otis Pike Wilderness Area, Fire Island Lighthouse, etc.)

- Other reason (please specify)

Respondents at the East End were lured by the quality and size of the beaches (61.5 percent) and the other attractions there, such as the Otis Pike Wilderness Area walkway (23.1 percent). Many respondents at the Lighthouse area were also attracted by the quality and size of the beaches (38.6 percent) and the Lighthouse and walkways (23.5 percent), but a sizeable number went because clothing optional bathing is permitted there (44.7 percent) and dogs are allowed (5.3 percent). A few of the other category comments indicated the FINS beaches were less crowded than the nearby state and county parks.

Table 4
Reasons for choosing FINS instead of nearby state and county parks
Source: Volpe Center, FINS Visitor Survey

Percent of Responses by Reason*	East End Visitors	West End Visitors	Total Visitors
Access to more, better beaches	61.5%	38.6%	45.1%
Access to more specific attractions	23.1%	23.5%	23.4%
Dogs permitted	0.0%	5.3%	3.8%
Clothing optional bathing permitted	0.0%	44.7%	32.1%
Other	25.0%	6.1%	11.4%

* Note: Respondents could choose more than one reason.

Paid parking

Table 5 shows that most respondents (61.5 percent overall) paid parking fees on the survey day; there was no significant difference between the two survey locations. These results show general agreement with Table 3 which indicates that overall 74.4 percent of respondents preferred to drive their own cars to the beach. One possible explanation, indicated by some comments, for the larger percentage that prefer to drive and the percentage that paid for parking is that some respondents had pre- paid parking passes.

Table 5
Respondents who paid for parking by location
Source: Volpe Center, FINS Visitor Survey

Pay		East End Visitors	West End Visitors	Total Visitors
Yes	Number	34	84	118
	% by Location	60.7%	61.8%	61.5%
No	Number	22	52	74
	% by Location	39.3%	38.2%	38.5%

Awareness of parking fee destination

In response to the question, *"Were you aware that the funds you paid for parking do not go to the National Seashore or to service the beach or other National Seashore area you are using?"* only about one quarter of the respondents replied in the affirmative. In contrast Question 1 above (Table 2) showed over 90 percent of respondents were aware they were entering a National Seashore on foot from the parking lots.

Table 6
Respondent awareness of parking fee destination
Source: Volpe Center, FINS Visitor Survey

Awareness		East End Visitors	West End Visitors	Total Visitors
Yes	Number	13	34	47
	% by Location	24.5%	25.4%	25.1%
No	Number	40	100	140
	% by Location	75.5%	74.6%	74.9%

Permanent residences of respondents

As shown in Table 7 almost 93 percent of survey respondents reside permanently in New York state. About 2 percent reside in New Jersey. Most of the remaining respondents live in east coast cities. A few respondents found their way to FINS from western states and foreign countries. Figure 6 shows the distribution of the residences of East End respondents by zip code. Figure 7 shows the residences of West End respondents. As expected, most of the respondents live on Long Island and in New York City, but the West End visitors come from a wider area, drawing more people from Manhattan and New Jersey than the East End.

Table 7
Permanent residences of respondents by state
Source: Volpe Center, FINS Visitor Survey

State and Country	East End Visitors	West End Visitors	Total Visitors
	Percent of Responses		
United States	96.2%	100.0%	99.4%
New York	90.4%	93.0%	92.8%
New Jersey	1.9%	2.3%	2.2%
West Virginia	0.0%	2.3%	1.7%
Connecticut	0.0%	1.6%	1.1%
Pennsylvania	1.9%	0.0%	0.6%
Texas	0.0%	0.8%	0.6%
California	1.9%	0.0%	0.6%
Scotland	1.9%	0.0%	0.6%

Figure 6
Permanent residences of East End respondents by zip code
Source: Volpe Center, FINS Visitor Survey

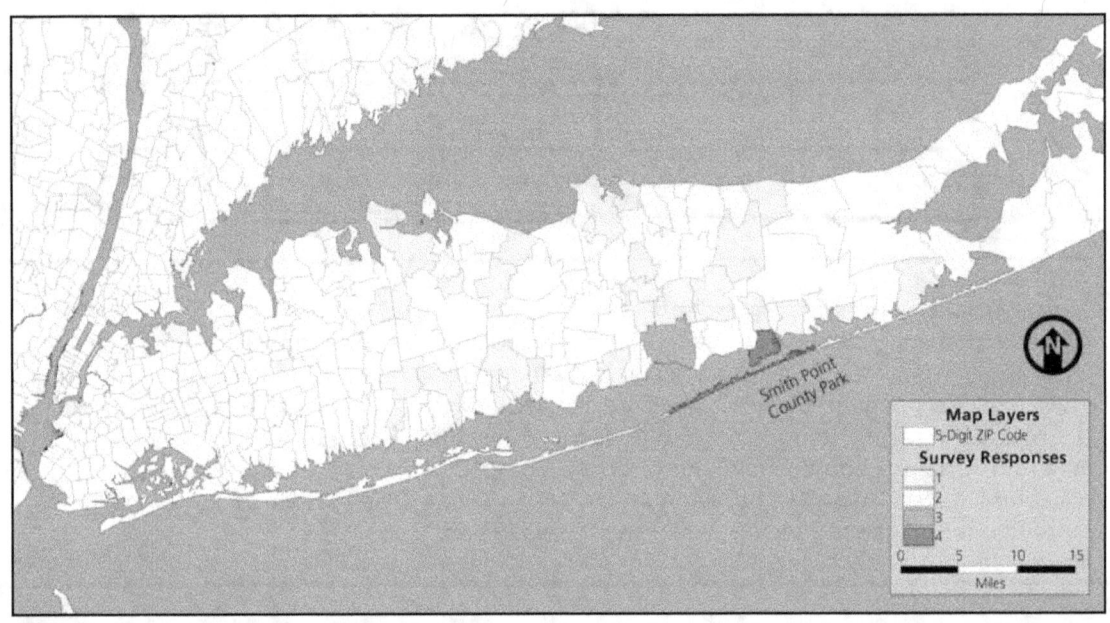

Figure 7
Permanent residences of West End respondents by zip code
Source: Volpe Center, FINS Visitor Survey

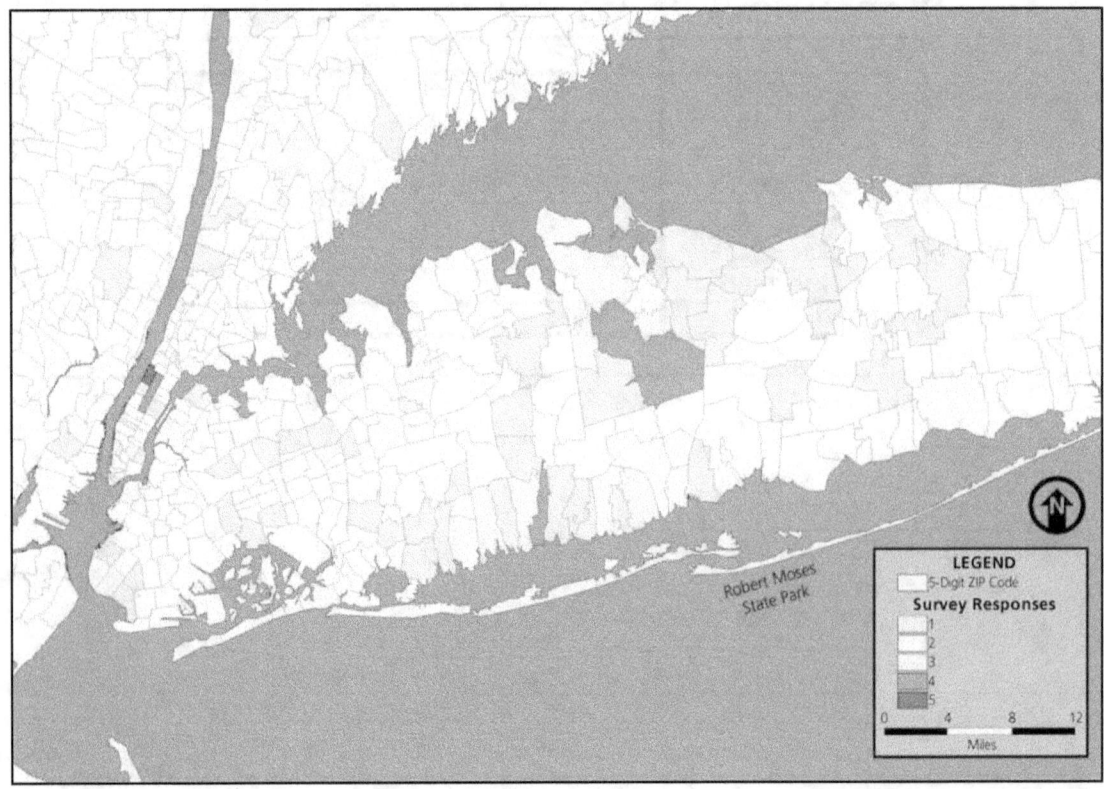

Travel party size

Table 8 shows that East End travel parties were somewhat larger than West End travel parties averaging 3.4 and 2.5 persons, respectively. The two-person travel party was the most common at 39.1 percent overall. About 18 percent of the travel parties included five or more people.

Table 8
Travel party size
Source: Volpe Center, FINS Visitor Survey

	East End Visitors	West End Visitors	Total Visitors
Survey Responses	56	136	192
Average Party Size	3.4	2.5	2.75
Percent of Responses by Location and Party Size			
1 Person	23.2%	30.9%	28.6%
2 Persons	28.6%	43.4%	39.1%
3 Persons	7.1%	5.9%	6.3%
4 Persons	12.5%	6.6%	8.3%
5 Persons	10.7%	5.1%	6.8%
6 Persons	12.5%	5.1%	7.3%
7 or More Persons	5.4%	2.9%	3.6%

Visitor ages

The "baby boomer" generation (45 – 65 years old) dominates the age range of visitors accessing FINS on foot at both locations: half of the West End visitors and around 30 percent of East End visitors are in this bracket. As mentioned earlier, survey Question 8 on travel party size did not include a bracket for party members 18 or less in age, and the table represents the data written in by some respondents. As a result, when viewing Table 9 readers should consider the percentages for the 18 or less bracket as minimums, i.e., at least 6.7 percent of East End visitors are 18 years or less. Other brackets should be interpreted as maximums, i.e., at most 43.6 percent of all visitors are in the 45 – 65 year old range.

Table 9
Ages of visitors
Source: Volpe Center, FINS Visitor Survey

Age Range	East End Visitors	West End Visitors	Total Visitors
	Percent by Location		
< 18 Years	6.7%	5.7%	6.0%
18 -- 24 Years	17.8%	3.4%	8.3%
25 -- 34 Years	14.4%	11.4%	12.4%
35 -- 44 Years	18.9%	27.8%	24.8%
45 -- 64 Years	31.1%	50.0%	43.6%
> or = 65 Years	11.1%	1.7%	4.9%

Respondent gender

Table 10 reveals that over two-thirds of respondents entering FINS on foot are male. As the questionnaire did not ask the gender of all members of the travel party, it is not possible to determine if this is reflective of the all on-foot visitors.

Table 10
Gender of respondents
Source: Volpe Center, FINS Visitor Survey

Sex of Respondent		East End Visitors	West End Visitors	Total Visitors
Female	Number	20	41	61
	% by Location	36.4%	32.0%	33.3%
Male	Number	35	87	122
	% by Location	63.6%	68.0%	66.7%

Household income

As reflected in Table 11, the pre- tax household incomes of visitors to both the East and West Ends of FINS are similarly distributed over the higher income ranges. For household incomes less than $50,000, respondents from the East End have lower incomes than those from the West End. On average, respondent household income was approximately $73,000.

Table 11
Household income of respondents
Source: Volpe Center, FINS Visitor Survey

Income Range	East End Visitors	West End Visitors	Total Visitors
	Percent by Location		
Number of Respondents	47	120	167
Under $25,000	14.9%	5.8%	8.4%
$25,000 to $49,999	14.9%	24.2%	21.6%
$50,000 to $74,999	25.5%	25.0%	25.1%
$75,000 to $99,999	19.1%	17.5%	18.0%
$100,000 or More	25.5%	27.5%	26.9%
Approximate Mean Income	$70,798	$73,729	$72,904

Feedback regarding possible new ferry routes

Question 12 presented respondents with a list of possible new ferry routes, and asked travelers to provided feedback regarding the potential desirability of these routes. The specific routes indicated on the survey instrument included:

- Bay Shore to Fire Island Lighthouse

- Sayville to Fire Island Lighthouse

- Heckscher State Park to Fire Island Lighthouse

- Patchogue to Fire Island Lighthouse

- Patchogue to Barrett Beach

- Heckscher State Park to Sailors Haven

- Lateral (east- west) water taxi service serving National Seashore areas

- Other route (specify)

Route options are presented in Figure 8 for reference. A response option indicating that the traveler felt that no new routes were needed and that existing routes were sufficient was also provided. The findings are presented in Table 12.

Although 83 of the 132 respondents that expressed an opinion felt the existing routes were sufficient, a number of respondents expressed a desire for more routes to the Fire Island Lighthouse: 16 respondents desired route to the Fire Island Lighthouse from Bay Shore; 10 desired a route from Heckscher State Park; 8 desired a route from Patchogue; and 4 desired a route from Sayville. They represented about 21 percent of the West End respondents and 18 percent of the East End respondents. Thirteen respondents had a favorable view of a ferry running coastwise along the northern shore of Fire Island. By way of contrast, the results of the companion Ferry Transportation Survey conducted in 2000 showed a strong preference for the coastwise ferry. The difference may lie in the length of stay of the respondents of the two surveys. Over 90 percent of respondents to this Visitor Survey were day- trippers, as parking is not allowed overnight, whereas almost three- quarters of respondents to the Ferry Transportation Survey stayed more than one day and might want to move about the island.

Table 12
Feedback regarding possible new ferry routes
Source: Volpe Center, FINS Visitor Survey

Preference for New Ferry Routes	East End Visitors	West End Visitors	Total Visitors
	Number of Favorable Responses		
Bay Shore - Fire Island Lighthouse	2	14	16
Coastwise East-West Ferry	3	10	13
Heckscher State Park - Fire Island Lighthouse	3	7	10
Patchogue - Fire Island Lighthouse	4	4	8
Sayville - Fire Island Lighthouse	1	3	4
Patchogue - Barrett Beach	2	1	3
Heckscher State Park - Sailor's Haven	1	1	2
Other Routes*	1	9	10
Existing Routes Sufficient	25	58	83

* Other suggested routes:
Sandy Hook to West End - 3 responses
Freeport to West End - 1 response
Manhattan to West End - 1 response

Figure 8
Potential new ferry routes presented to FINS Visitor Survey respondents
Source: Volpe Center, FINS Visitor Survey

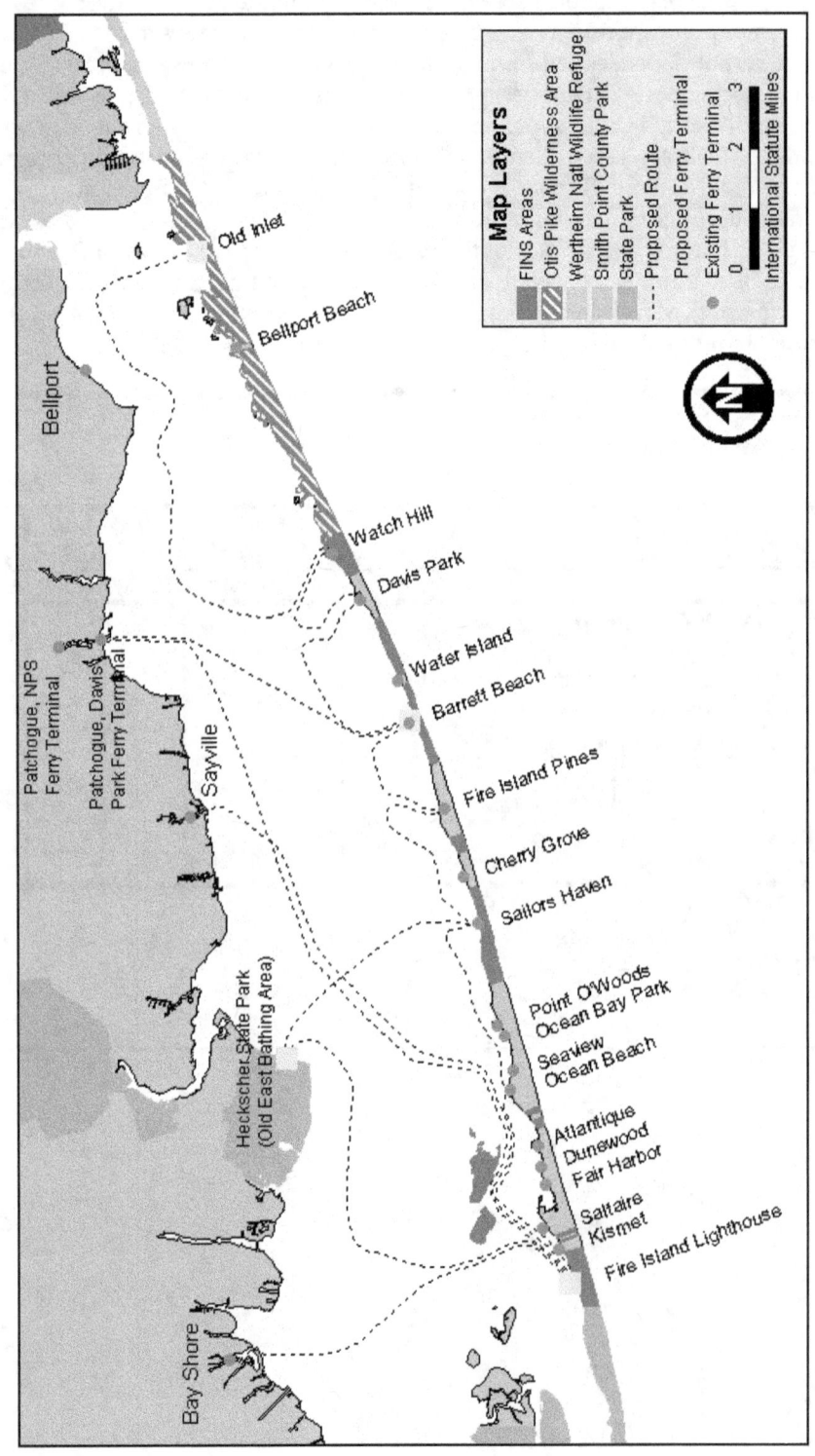

General comments

Table 13 summarizes the comments received from the backside of the Visitor Survey in the comment section provided, broken down by location, subject area and nature of the comment. Comments received from East End visitors were generally positive, showing appreciation for the quality of the beach and park, and the helpfulness of the rangers there. While many West End visitors also appreciated the quality of the beach and park, even more expressed a desire for more trash cans and bathrooms, and a greater beach area allocated for clothing optional use.

Table 13
General comments by location and nature
Source: Volpe Center, FINS Visitor Survey

Subject of Comment	East End Visitors		West End Visitors	
	Positive Comments	Negative Comments	Positive Comments	Negative Comments
Beach/park quality	4	1	11	0
Beach cleanliness	1	0	0	2
Ranger helpfulness	4	0	0	0
Environmental protection efforts	1	1	0	2
Parking availability	0	2	0	1
Road/bridge access to beaches	0	0	0	3
Trash can availability	0	0	0	14
Bathroom availability	0	0	0	3
Dogs on beaches	0	0	1	2
SUVs on beaches	0	0	0	1
Size of clothing optional beach	0	0	0	5
Life guard protection	0	0	0	1
Other	0	1	2	0

Section 4: Summary

The FINS Visitor Survey provided useful insights into the travel needs of visitors walking into the East and West Ends of FINS and their characteristics.

The Fire Island Visitor Survey was conducted on July 27 and 28 at two locations on Fire Island. In the East, surveyors intercepted visitors as they walked into the Otis Pike Wilderness Area of FINS, and in the West, surveyors intercepted visitors as they walked into the Fire Island Lighthouse area and beach. Although the weather did not cooperate, 192 surveys in all were collected from visitors to the areas, providing a large enough sample for representative statistical results.

The vast majority of respondents did realize that they were visiting a unit of the National Park Service, rather than state or county parks. They came to FINS primarily because of the quality of the beaches and attractions, although a significant number visiting the Lighthouse beach came because of the clothing optional policy.

Residing mainly in the New York City area or on Long Island, day visitors largely preferred to drive their own cars to the island and walk into FINS. Most paid parking fees, but did not realize the fees did not go to the National Seashore. On average, they came in groups of two to three people. Almost half of them were "baby boomers," and two-thirds were males. Mean pre-tax income was high at around $73,000.

While the majority of respondents felt the existing ferry routes were sufficient, approximately 20 percent of those who expressed an opinion desired ferry routes to the Fire Island Lighthouse from various points on Long Island. Respondents showed some interest in a coastwise ferry along the northern shore of Fire Island, but not as much as respondents to a prior survey in 2000, the FINS Ferry Transportation Survey, administered to riders of ferries to Fire Island.

Appendices

Two appendices accompany this report:

- *Appendix A is the Visitor Survey Expedited Approval Form*

- *Appendix B is the instructions for surveyors to conduct the survey*

Appendix A. National Park Service Expedited Approval Form for Visitor Survey

According to the Paperwork Reduction Act of 1995, before a survey involving more than ten persons can occur, a federal agency must obtain approval from OMB. To expedite the approval process, the National Park Service has developed an internal vetting process through its Social Service Program for survey approval packages prior to submitting them to OMB. The internal review process and survey documentation requirements are laid out in the NPS publication *Guidelines and Approval Form for Expedited Approval for NPS- sponsored Public Surveys* (December 2001). The Visitor Survey's survey instrument and survey methodology conformed to these guidelines and were approved in August 2000. This appendix contains the FINS Visitor Survey approval package.

Project Title Submission Date:	Fire Island National Seashore Visitor Study	7/28/2000

Abstract: Fire Island National Seashore (FINS) represents a unique situation relevant to transportation needs, given its lack of access via conventional ground transport modes and services. There are no direct bridge connections to the federally-managed portions of Fire Island, and approximately 80% to 90% of the estimated 3 to 4 million annual visitors to the federally-managed portions of Fire Island access the Island by either ferry or private boat. This survey is being conducted by FINS to help determine how ferry service to FINS can be improved. The information gathered from visitors who currently access FINS on foot from nearby Robert Moses State Park and Smith Point County Park, rather than by ferry, will aid in the development of a waterborne transportation plan aimed at improving public access to, and use and enjoyment of, the resources of FINS.

(not to exceed 150 words)

Principal Investigator Contact Information

First Name: Robert **Last Name:** Armstrong

Title: Economist

Affiliation: U.S. Dept. of Transportation, Volpe Center

Street Address: 55 Broadway (DTS-42)

City: Cambridge **State:** MA **Zip code:** 02142

Phone: (617) 494-2946 **Fax:** (617) 494-2787

Email: armstrongr@volpe.dot.gov

Park or Program Liaison Contact Information

First Name: Constantine **Last Name:** Dillon

Title: Superintendent

Park: Fire Island National Seashore

Park Office/Division: Headquarters

Street Address: 120 Laurel Street

roject Information

5. **Park(s) Where Research is Conducted:** Fire Island National Seashore

6. **Survey Dates:** 09/9/2000 (mm/dd/yyyy) to 09/9/2000 (mm/dd/yyyy)

7. **Type of Information Collection Instrument (Check all that Apply)**

    ❑ Mail Survey   X On-site Survey   ❑ Interview   ❑ Focus Groups

    ❑ Other (explain)

8. **Survey Justification:** (Use as much space as needed; if necessary include additional explanation on a separate page.)

Despite the fact that ferry transportation is critically important for public access to, and use and enjoyment of, the resources of FINS, even basic information concerning ferry trip characteristics and ferry rider characteristics in the area are currently unknown. This survey will provide critical and otherwise unavailable information that will help guide the decision making process in developing possible modifications to existing ferry services and/or facilities, and the possible introduction of new ferry services and/or facilities, in order to improve public access to, and use and enjoyment of, the resources of FINS. Weekends (Saturday - Sunday) during the summer season represent the heaviest periods of visitation to FINS and to the nearby state and county parks, and it is thought that there is no significant systematic variation in the characteristics of the visitor population on Saturdays versus Sundays. Therefore, implementing the survey on a single Saturday will sample a respondent universe that is representative of a large proportion of all visitors to FINS (i.e., weekend summer visitors). In addition, this large number of weekend visitors represents a significant potential source of patronage for alternative travel modes, such as new or improved ferry services, that could be used by FINS visitors who currently drive and park at the nearby state and county parks.

9. **Survey Methodology:** (Use as much space as needed; if necessary include additional explanation on a separate page.)

(see attached page)

| **Total Number of Initial Contacts\| Expected Respondents:** | 300 | 150 | 11. | **Estimated Time to Complete Initial Contact\| Instrument (mins.):** | .25 | 5 | 12. | **Total Burden Hours:** | 13.75 |

Survey Methodology

Respondent Universe

The respondent universe is all visitors age 18 and older to Fire Island National Seashore (FINS) who access FINS on foot from either Robert Moses State Park to the west, or Smith Point County Park to the east, during the survey period of one Saturday during the peak visitation season. Weekends (Saturday - Sunday) during the summer season represent the heaviest periods of visitation to FINS and to the nearby state and county parks, and it is thought that there is no significant systematic variation in the characteristics of the visitor population on Saturdays versus Sundays. Therefore, implementing the survey on a single Saturday will sample a respondent universe that is representative of a large proportion of all visitors to FINS (i.e., weekend summer visitors). In addition, this large number of weekend visitors represents a significant potential source of patronage for alternative travel modes, such as new or improved ferry services, that could be used by FINS visitors who currently drive and park at the nearby state and county parks.

Sampling Plan and Sampling Procedures

On a typical Saturday during the peak visitation season, it is estimated that approximately 3,000 visitors to the Fire Island National Seashore (FINS) access the park on foot from Robert Moses State Park to the west, and 1,500 visitors access FINS on foot from Smith Point County Park to the east. Of this total respondent universe of 4,500 visitors who access FINS by foot from nearby parks, a sample of 300 visitors (200 entering from Robert Moses State Park and 100 entering from Smith Point County Park) will be selected throughout the day at access points along the beach and along the boardwalks, and will be contacted by FINS staff or Volpe Center staff and asked to participate in the survey. A systematic sampling approach will be utilized, in which every n^{th} person at each access point will be selected. There is no reason to believe that such a sampling order is biased, therefore this approach is essentially equivalent to a simple random sample.

Survey Administration

On the Saturday that the survey is administered, there will be four survey field workers in total, two at each of the state and county parks, one intercepting visitors gaining access to FINS along the beach and the other intercepting visitors gaining access to FINS along the boardwalk.

The surveyors will use the following greeting:

> *Good morning/afternoon. The National Park Service is conducting a brief visitor survey today in cooperation with (state or county park name). The survey, which is being conducted to help determine how access to Fire Island can be improved, is voluntary and all responses are confidential. Would you be willing to participate?* **If Yes:** *Thank you.* **If No:** *Enjoy your trip to Fire Island.*

Survey instruments will be secured to clip boards, and a writing implement will be provided to the respondent. Completed surveys will be collected by the surveyor and placed into a secure water resistant bag carried by the surveyor for safe keeping.

Expected Response Rate

Considering that each member of the respondent universe will be greeted by a surveyor, an overall response rate of about 50% is anticipated.

Non- Response Bias

For this survey, the main source of non- response that may occur is if a visitor refuses to participate in the survey when initially approached by the surveyor. For those initial contacts that decline to participate, the surveyor will note observable characteristics such as gender, an estimate of group size and an estimate of age. In an attempt to identify any systematic distortion in survey responses that may result if the survey respondents are different than the survey non- respondents, a comparison will be made between the proportion of visitors in each sex, age and group size category for the non-respondents, and the proportion of visitors in each sex, age and group size category for those who participate in the survey. If substantial differences are found between these proportions, the resulting information may be used to weight the survey responses to more accurately reflect actual conditions in the respondent universe.

Appendix B. FINS Visitor Survey Instructions

Materials each surveyor will need:

- Signs: "Survey Today" sign; "Deposit Completed Surveys Here" sign

- Surveys - - 60 per surveyor at the East End (Smith Point) and 110 per surveyor at the West End (Robert Moses)

- Box for completed survey returns - - "Collection Box"

- Two chairs from the nearest FINS facility

- Golf pencils

- 4 clipboards

- Tape, magic marker, pushpins, pens, clipboard

- Script for addressing prospective participants

- Nonresponse bias check form

- National Park identification badge

- Uniform or neat white shirt, any color shorts or slacks, shoes or sandals

- Suntan lotion, hat, water

- Cell phone

- Backpack or such for lugging this stuff around, or maybe it will fit into the Collection Box

Instructions:
SET UP

- Identify yourself to the ***Park Rangers or other official types***, and remind them you'll be conducting the survey all day.

- Locate a ***place for you to stand (your station) on FINS property*** to greet survey participants as they approach FINS. At both the East and West sites, one surveyor should stand at the main walkway into FINS, the other at the beginning of the beach to intercept people walking into FINS via the beach. Stage the survey forms, golf pencils, and clipboards nearby. Insert survey forms on the clipboards ahead of time.

- Set up the "***Survey Today" sign*** in a location with good visibility to people approaching FINS.

- Locate the main way people will be leaving FINS (likely the same way they came in), and set up the ***box for completed survey forms***, the "Deposit Completed Surveys Here" sign, and a small box for golf pencil return.

- ***Practice the scripted greeting*** (below) so you don't have to read it every time you approach a prospective respondent.

CONDUCT THE SURVEY - - 8AM - 4PM

- **_Situate yourself at your station_** to greet people as they approach FINS.

- Approach every **_fifteenth_** (1/15) adult 18 and over, and use the scripted greeting (below) to ask him or her to participate in the survey. Use your best judgment to estimate if a person is 18 or older. Do not count children under 18. If the person has already taken the survey at another location (very unlikely!), go to the very next person - - do not wait for the fifteenth. Keep count of the number of people in this category throughout the day.

- **_If the person you approach declines to participate_**, but another person in his/her travel party volunteers (i.e., he/she overhears and comes forward voluntarily - - you do not ask him/her), you can **_give the volunteer the survey form_**. Do not fill in a line in the Nonresponse Bias Check form.

- If no one else in the travel party comes forward, or if the original person is traveling alone, then **_fill in the Nonresponse Bias Check_** form (see instructions below for filling in this form), and count the next 15 people to reach the next prospect, and approach him/her.

- **_Hand willing participants a survey form_**, and offer them a golf pencil. Offer them a clipboard if they wish to complete it on the spot - encourage this option. Offer them a chair or bench. Point out the collection box, and let them know you're available if they have questions about the survey during the day, etc.

- Each surveyor at the East End should expect to **_distribute_** approximately 50 surveys at his/her station for the day, and each surveyor at the West End 100. (About 10 extra surveys are in your material packages for rips, mistakes, etc). You should remain at your stations until all surveys are distributed, or until 4PM.

- As you see people depositing the completed forms into the collection box, thank them for participating, or **_accept the completed survey forms_** if they just hand them to you.

SHIFT CHANGES

- Inform your replacement of the **_procedures_** you have been following, and any necessary modifications due to weather, unforeseen circumstances, etc.

- Inform the replacement of any **_problems_** you have encountered.

BREAKS

- If you are working approximately a four- hour shift, please **_limit your bathroom or snack breaks to 15 minutes_** at a time. If you are working a longer shift, please limit your meal break to 30 minutes.

- The person on duty around lunchtime should **_check in at the designated telephone number_** to report on your progress and any problems you may be encountering. You may contact this number at any time if there is an emergency or a serious problem.

AT 4PM

- **_Gather up the survey materials_** at your station (extra survey forms, clipboards, golf pencils, "Survey Today" sign, etc.).

- *Remove completed survey forms from the boxes*, clip them together or place them in a container, *mark the date and location* on a sheet of paper, and attach it to the pile of surveys. Return the forms, and all other materials to the designated place - - tbd.

- *Leave the Collection Boxes in place* for people who have taken the form to the beach with them and are leaving after 4PM. Someone will come by later to pick up the boxes.

The Script

Good morning/afternoon/evening. The National Park Service is conducting a brief transportation survey today in cooperation with [Smith Point County Park] or [Robert Moses State Park]. The survey, which is being conducted to help determine how access to Fire Island can be improved, is voluntary, and all responses are confidential. Would you be willing to participate?

If no: Enjoy your trip to Fire Island [End of contact - - go to next person.]

If yes: Thank you! Would you like to complete it here - - it will take only a couple of minutes. Or you can take it with you, fill it out on the beach, and return it to the Collection Box here [point to the location of the box].

Completing the Nonresponse Bias Check Form

Gender		Age Estimate					Group Size
Male	Female	18 to 24	25 to 34	35 to 44	45 to 64	65 or over	

This form is to be completed when a person you approach (or his entire travel party) refuses to take the survey. It is not to be completed for people who have already taken the survey at another location. You need to input the person's gender, your best guess of his/her age, and the group size. When the entire travel party has refused to take the survey, just enter the information about the first person you approached.

REPORT DOCUMENTATION PAGE

Form Approved
OMB No. 0704-0188

The public reporting burden for this collection of information is estimated to average 1 hour per response, including the time for reviewing instructions, searching existing data sources, gathering and maintaining the data needed, and completing and reviewing the collection of information. Send comments regarding this burden estimate or any other aspect of this collection of information, including suggestions for reducing the burden, to Department of Defense, Washington Headquarters Services, Directorate for Information Operations and Reports (0704-0188), 1215 Jefferson Davis Highway, Suite 1204, Arlington, VA 22202-4302. Respondents should be aware that notwithstanding any other provision of law, no person shall be subject to any penalty for failing to comply with a collection of information if it does not display a currently valid OMB control number.
PLEASE DO NOT RETURN YOUR FORM TO THE ABOVE ADDRESS.

1. REPORT DATE (DD-MM-YYYY)	2. REPORT TYPE	3. DATES COVERED (From - To)
30-AP-2005	Planning Study	NA

4. TITLE AND SUBTITLE

Fire Island National Seashore Survey of Walk-in Visitors

5a. CONTRACT NUMBER

NA

5b. GRANT NUMBER

NA

5c. PROGRAM ELEMENT NUMBER

NA

6. AUTHOR(S)

Judith C. Schwenk, Principal Author
Robert A. Armstrong
Michael Dyer, Project Leader

5d. PROJECT NUMBER

PMIS 63642

5e. TASK NUMBER

NPS TIC No. D-95

5f. WORK UNIT NUMBER

NA

7. PERFORMING ORGANIZATION NAME(S) AND ADDRESS(ES)

John A. Volpe National Transportation Systems Center
Research and Innovative Technology Administration
U. S. Department of Transportation
55 Broadway, Cambridge, MA 02142

8. PERFORMING ORGANIZATION REPORT NUMBER

DOT-VNTSC-NPS-05-15

9. SPONSORING/MONITORING AGENCY NAME(S) AND ADDRESS(ES)

National Park Service
Alternative Transportation Program
1201 Eye St. NW
Washington, DC 20005

10. SPONSOR/MONITOR'S ACRONYM(S)

WASO/ATP

11. SPONSOR/MONITOR'S REPORT NUMBER(S)

(see 5d. and 5e. above)

12. DISTRIBUTION/AVAILABILITY STATEMENT

Public distribution/availability.

13. SUPPLEMENTARY NOTES

This report addresses alternative transportation decision factors as indicated below (Y/N/NA):
(Y) Non-construction options; (N) park carrying capacity; (N) life-cycle/ops. & maintenance costs; (N) cost-effectiveness.

14. ABSTRACT

The FINS Survey of Walk-in Visitors was conducted with the aim of determining how public access to the island can be improved. This survey obtained input from visitors who access the National Seashore on foot from nearby Robert Moses State Park on the East End of FINS and Smith Point County Park on the West End. The information will aid FINS in further developing its waterborne transportation plan for the improvement of public access to, and use and enjoyment of, FINS resources. This effort continues work initiated and documented in the February 2001 Phase I report, Fire Island National Seashore Waterborne Transportation System Plan, in which the Volpe Center identified ferry and water taxi service and terminal improvements to be phased in from 2001-2010. The project statement of work was conducted in cooperation with the Federal Highway Administration (FHWA) under Volpe Center/FHWA Project Plan Agreement HW1M as a supplement to PMIS 63642.

15. SUBJECT TERMS

national park, park, alternative transportation, transportation, visitor experience, ferry transportation

16. SECURITY CLASSIFICATION OF:			17. LIMITATION OF ABSTRACT	18. NUMBER OF PAGES	19a. NAME OF RESPONSIBLE PERSON
a. REPORT	b. ABSTRACT	c. THIS PAGE			
None	None	None	NA	29	19b. TELEPHONE NUMBER (Include area code)

Reset

Standard Form 298 (Rev. 8/98)
Prescribed by ANSI Std. Z39.18

www.ingramcontent.com/pod-product-compliance
Lightning Source LLC
Chambersburg PA
CBHW080353290526
45791CB00009BA/2859